STRONGER THAN THE STORM –

THE LAST WORDS OF JESUS

AND BONUS BOOK: PICTURES OF SALVATION

BRIAN JOHNSTON

Copyright © 2013 Hayes Press

Published by:

HAYES PRESS CHRISTIAN PUBLISHERS

The Barn, Flaxlands

Royal Wootton Bassett

Swindon, SN4 8DY

United Kingdom

www.hayespress.org

CHAPTER ONE: FATHER, FORGIVE THEM

It was a memorable afternoon as we sat together as a group, sharing God's Word. About fifteen to twenty of us had gathered under the porch of a house in the tropics. There was a good-natured atmosphere, which made the time spent there immensely enjoyable, but what was most thrilling was a real sense that God's Word was being received as the voice of the living God. Here was a group engaging with the Bible as the Word of God. The sounds of a neighbour's karaoke machine and a passing rain-shower weren't sufficient to distract us that afternoon. Questions came pouring out, and again and again we turned to the most relevant Bible verses and found answers that truly satisfied hearts that were seriously thirsty. Finally, the lady, under whose porch we were sheltering from the heat, exclaimed, "It's magnificent!"

It truly is a magnificent experience whenever we hear God's voice speaking to our heart out of our reading of his Word, the Bible. In the days which followed, the unfolding of events clearly confirmed that a work of God's Holy Spirit really had taken place in the hearts of our host family, and days of rejoicing followed just like we read about in the New Testament. But that unsolicited remark extolling the magnificence of God's voice in his Word remained with me afterwards, and reminded me of Psalm 29 - a psalm which graphically describes for us the voice of the Lord. Let me remind you of what it says:

"The voice of the LORD is upon the waters;

The God of glory thunders, The LORD is over many waters.

The voice of the LORD is powerful,

The voice of the LORD is majestic.

The voice of the LORD breaks the cedars;

Yes, the LORD breaks in pieces the cedars of Lebanon.

He makes Lebanon skip like a calf,

And Sirion like a young wild ox.

The voice of the LORD hews out flames of fire.

The voice of the LORD shakes the wilderness;

The LORD shakes the wilderness of Kadesh.

The voice of the LORD makes the deer to calve

And strips the forests bare;

And in His temple everything says, "Glory!"

(Psalm 29:3-29)

These words themselves are magnificent. They give us a breathtaking illustration of the power and majesty of the Lord's voice set over against the background picture of a breaking storm. It's certainly possible (indeed, it's likely) that David had been watching a storm approaching the land of Israel from out over the Mediterranean Sea when the words of this psalm came to him. Picture this storm as David describes it approaching with its 'many waters': there's darkness and lightning; thunder and earth-shakings; waves rising and leaves falling. It's as if we follow the storm inland, across and down the land of Israel. And this noisy storm, which displays God's power and majesty in creation, makes David think of the power and majesty of the voice of the Lord - the very voice which spoke the world into existence.

But it also reminded David of the fact that God's in control of the storm. Seven times he mentions 'the voice of the Lord' - as being on the waters; as being powerful; as being majestic as breaking trees; as making flames of fire; as shaking the desert; and as making the forest bare - seven reminders that the voice of the Lord really is magnificent, and is over all and in all. Some countries, for example in the tropics, know all about storms. But there are other kinds of storms too. It's in the storms of life that God's voice can sound most powerful and majestic to us. In storms of doubt and despair; when our way seems dark; and our beliefs are shaken, and we're stripped of our hopes, how magnificent it is when we hear the sound of the Lord's voice in our reading of his Word. Remember, what the Bible says - God says (e.g. compare Romans 9:17 & Exodus 9:16).

God's Word changes lives; it did mine. I'd like you to imagine you're out walking. The night is dark and you're all alone. Suddenly, you turn around to see ten strong men coming towards you! Then you notice that each one of them is carrying a Bible. Wouldn't that make a difference to how you feel? The Word of God makes a difference! God is stronger than any storm, and we've moved on to consider various kinds of storms in our lives. I would now like to take this a stage further in relating it to the experience of Jesus Christ. The world became dark on the Friday Jesus died on the cross around 2,000 years ago. The Bible describes Jesus' experience there in terms of a storm breaking over him - and that was the greatest storm ever. Listen to this description from another psalm in our Bibles, this time from Psalm 69. As you read the words, try to relate them to Jesus dying on the cross, crying out in his agony:

"Save me, O God,

For the waters have threatened my life.

I have sunk in deep mire, and there is no foothold;

I have come into deep waters, and a flood overflows me.

I am weary with my crying; my throat is parched;

My eyes fail while I wait for my God.

Those who hate me without a cause are more than the hairs of my head;

Those who would destroy me are powerful, being wrongfully my enemies;

What I did not steal, I then have to restore."

(Psalm 69:1-4)

Sin had robbed us of our relationship with God, but Jesus, God's own Son, had come to make its restoration possible for any one of us. Psalm 69 with its waves and deep waters is one of the Bible's poetic and graphic descriptions which we can take as having an application to Jesus when he died for our sins (1 Corinthians 15:3). For it was then he was baptized in floods of death, when the waves of God's judgement against sin broke over him: the innocent, sinless substitute who had been provided as part of God's plan to bring salvation to everyone who believes on him. Seven times in association with that great storm of the cross, the voice of the Lord was heard, reminding us of the seven mentions of 'the voice of the Lord' in Psalm 29 in the middle of the storm described there. You'll remember how we said that the marvelous word picture of the development of a great storm there is punctuated seven times by 'the voice of the Lord'. In this booklet, I'd like us to consider each of the seven sayings of our Saviour from out of the terrible storm of Calvary where he died. We begin with the first of those seven cries from the cross, which we read about in Luke chapter 23: "When they came to the place called The Skull, there they crucified Him and the criminals, one on the right and the other on the left. But Jesus was saying, "Father, forgive them; for they do not know what they are doing." And they cast lots, dividing up His garments among themselves" (Luke 23:33-34).

Obviously, this is the scene of the crucifixion. Jesus' days of moving about among the people, his days of teaching and healing were at an end, for his hands and feet - those hands which had done such good - were now nailed to the cross. He could no longer travel on errands of mercy, but what he could do, he did: he turned to the ministry of prayer on behalf of others. We pause here just to say that, as you listen, you may be someone who doesn't have freedom of movement any longer, perhaps as a result: of advancing age or because of the onset of illness. Pease don't feel that there's nothing useful you can do now; instead, follow our Lord's wonderful example of engaging in a ministry of prayer for others.

In praying like this for those who abused him, the Lord was fulfilling his own teaching, for he had previously said: "Bless those who curse you, pray for those who mistreat you" (Luke 6:28). This was a masterful example of practising in our own lives what we preach to others. Previously, Jesus had pronounced forgiveness - as in the case of the paralyzed man. On that occasion, recorded in Mark's gospel, chapter 2, he'd said to the paralytic, "Son, your sins are forgiven" (v.5). But now, here on the cross, he prays to his Father in heaven to forgive them. Why the difference? Is it because here at the cross, Jesus, though still the Son of God, was now our representative, identifying with us so that he might, in the will of God, die the just for the unjust that he might bring us to God (1 Peter 3:18)?

The Lord was praying for those who did not know what they were doing. The law of God in the Old Testament had underlined the seriousness of sin in God's estimate, by demanding that even sins committed in ignorance had to be dealt with (e.g. Leviticus 4:2). Ignorance is no excuse. Those who nailed Jesus Christ to that shameful cross were not aware of the enormity of what they were doing: imagine crucifying the Lord of glory! Satan still blinds the minds of the unbelieving today to prevent them from seeing the glory of God in the face of Jesus

Christ (2 Corinthians 4:4) - and from seeing what the cross, in reality, is all about. But this blind ignorance is no excuse. The Lord's prayer shows such sins also require to be forgiven. Think about that. As the storm was about to break, the Lord's voice was heard in prayer - and what a prayer! And what a magnificent Saviour! - one who is now risen as the living Word of God! Today, if you hear his voice, do not harden your hearts (Hebrews 4:7).

CHAPTER TWO: WITH ME IN PARADISE

I remember one night lying in bed as a tropical storm broke overhead. I don't know if it was the noise of the storm which woke me or the fact that I was getting wet! Rainwater was pouring down the wall of the room. The friendly hotel staff member was very helpful - he assisted me in pulling the bed out a few centimeters further away from the wall, so at least I didn't get wet. It's a different class of service you get in some parts of the world!

There's something awesome about a terrific storm: something to do with the display of raw power. In this book we'll keep referring back to Psalm 29 - a psalm which graphically describes for us the voice of the Lord. Let's remind ourselves of what it says:

"The voice of the LORD is upon the waters;

The God of glory thunders, The LORD is over many waters.

The voice of the LORD is powerful,

The voice of the LORD is majestic.

The voice of the LORD breaks the cedars;

Yes, the LORD breaks in pieces the cedars of Lebanon.

He makes Lebanon skip like a calf,

And Sirion like a young wild ox.

The voice of the LORD hews out flames of fire.

The voice of the LORD shakes the wilderness;

The LORD shakes the wilderness of Kadesh.

The voice of the LORD makes the deer to calve

And strips the forests bare;

And in His temple everything says, "Glory!"

(Psalm 29:3-9)

The storm, that David seems to have been watching, reminded him that God's in control - even in the storms of life. Seven times he mentions 'the voice of the Lord' - as being on the waters; as being powerful; as being majestic as breaking trees; as making flames of fire as shaking the desert; and as making the forest bare - in total seven reminders that the voice of the Lord is magnificent. There are other kinds of storms too. In the storms of life God's voice can sound equally powerful and majestic The Bible makes reference to what it calls 'the treasures of darkness'. I'd like to apply that phrase today to something we can all possess - something which can be ours because God's Son, Jesus, came to a dark place, so we could have this treasure. The world became dark when Jesus died on the cross. The Bible describes Jesus as enduring a great storm there: with waves of suffering breaking over him (Psalm 69). Seven times the voice of the Lord Jesus was heard from the cross, the cross where the greatest ever storm broke. And now we come to the second of the seven times the Lord's voice was heard. We'll let the gospel writer, Luke, bring it to us from his gospel, chapter 23:

> "One of the criminals who were hanged there was hurling abuse at Him, saying, "Are You not the Christ? Save Yourself and us!' But the other answered, and rebuking him said, "Do you not even fear God, since you are under the same sentence of condemnation? And we indeed are suffering justly, for we are receiving what we deserve for our deeds; but this man has done nothing wrong." And he was saying, "Jesus, remember me when You come in Your kingdom!" And He said to him, "Truly I say to you, today you shall be with Me in Paradise" (Luke 23:39-43).

Yes, this is Christ's word spoken to the dying thief. It tells the story of an eleventh hour conversion - recorded to demonstrate that we're saved by faith, and not by works. For what works could a man do who was bound hand and foot to a cross? But equally, this record of how one of the thieves received salvation proves how essential genuine repentance is for anyone who wants to be saved. Notice the thief's unqualified confession: "We are receiving what we deserve for our deeds." Unlike his accomplice in crime who was crucified on the other side of Jesus, this man no longer screams abuse or demands to be freed from this punishment he's experiencing. He admits he's getting what he deserves. There are no more excuses, nor any appeals for sympathy - just an acceptance of guilt on his part.

Hanging next to Christ in death, this man's whole way of thinking underwent a profound change. That's what the Bible means by repentance. The dying thief s view of himself and of his past deeds has changed, but so has his view of Christ. He's stopped joining in with the mockery. Remember, this man has lived a lawless life, one which has opposed the rule of law. His had been a life of obvious rebel lion, defying the government of the day as a political activist or murderous bandit - or perhaps both. Fair play was something he'd never had any respect for.

But, now, see the effect of his repentance. He's done with anarchy: he's applying to be admitted to the kingdom of Christ! He's willingly yielding to his rue and authority, while fully recognizing Christ's right to reign over him. The Bible says we all need to repent. Even if we've been law-abiding citizens in our relations with our country, for it's been a different story in our relations with God. The Bible doesn't charge us all with serious crimes, but it does charge us all with 'going astray' from God. Every one of us. We've turned, every one, to his own way, the prophet Isaiah says. And what God requires is repentance: which is that we, the unrighteous, forsake our thoughts - our own wicked and rebellious thoughts - and return to the Lord.

This world is in the mess it's in, because we all go about acting like little gods, trying to take charge of our own lives. The dying thief had done that big time. But he was through with it. He was handing over the reins of his life to Christ - at the eleventh hour.

The dying thief had not only repented of his sin, but had also placed his faith in Christ. But you may say: "How?" He didn't say, "I believe." No, but he spoke of Christ's future kingdom. That took faith, for Christ was dying at his side. Evidently, he'd come to believe that, despite Christ dying on the cross at that moment, he would one day come again to reign. What might have inspired such faith in this God-fearing thief? Had he heard the Lord's first cry from the cross - the one we considered in the previous chapter of the book - when he'd prayed a prayer of forgiveness for those who had driven the nails into his hands and feet? Surely here was evidence not only of innocence but of unearthly goodness! How could anyone pray for those who were so brutally abusing him? Had that been the point when the thief, witnessing it, had at last began to care about the difference between right and wrong?

"In our case we deserved it," he heard himself say. "But this man has done nothing wrong." As the penny was dropping for him, it might have seemed too little, too late. He realized he'd done wrong, surely many wrongs. He needed to get right with God. But how could that happen now. Surely, he'd left; it too late. Any resolution to reform his ways was a waste of his dying breath. Besides, the pain shooting through his body was a disincentive to prayer, and he was likely a complete stranger to prayer anyway. What could he do, but turn, as a poor, broken rebel to Christ. If those soldiers could be forgiven because they didn't know the enormity of what they were doing, surely he could be forgiven - he, who had never realized before how wonderful God's King really was - until being nailed alongside him. He'd never intended to rebel against a king like that - like the man crucified next to him with the superscription: 'This is Jesus, the king of the Jews'. So at the end of his life, a self-confessed anarchist bowed his heart in faith to heaven's King - and was at once assured of admittance into that coming kingdom.

We're never told his previous partner in crime turned to Christ, we're left to assume that he departed this life to face the judgement to come; whereas this thief departed to enjoy the kingdom to come – and more than that to be in Paradise with Christ that very same day! How full of majesty was the voice of the Lord that day: "Today you shall be with Me in Paradise." As supernatural darkness was about to descend at noon that day, and the storm about to break in earnest over Jesus, hearing those words of Jesus was treasure beyond anything the repentant thief could ever have hoped for! Treasures of darkness indeed! Have you received treasure like that? Even the forgiveness of sins by repenting and believing on the sacrifice of God's Son for you?

CHAPTER THREE: BEHOLD YOUR MOTHER

The Lord had been in physical storms on the Sea of Galilee with his disciples. One time they had wakened him in fear for their lives while he was asleep in the stern of a storm-tossed boat. On that occasion, he'd risen up and given a command to the wind and the waves, and they'd obeyed him. No wonder the disciples had asked: "What kind of man is this, that even the winds and the waves obey him!" The voice of the Lord had been upon the waters as a powerful voice, a majestic voice - just like we read in Psalm 29.

But it was an altogether different tempest that raged at Calvary, where Jesus died. While Jesus hung there, the greatest storm ever broke over him. Not a physical storm, but the storm of God's wrath, God's anger against sin, while he, Jesus, the Son of God, was there as the Lamb of God to bear away the sin of the world (John 1:29). There, Christ died for his creature's sins, according to the Bible (1 Corinthians 15:3). He suffered there as no one has ever suffered, and seven times from the cross the Saviour's voice was heard. In our study we come to the third of these sayings, the one in which Christ addressed the disciple, John, and his mother, Mary. We'll let John himself tell us about the exchange from his record found in John's Gospel, chapter 19:

> "... standing by the cross of Jesus were His mother, and His mother's sister, Mary the wife of Clopas, and Mary Magdalene. When Jesus then saw His mother, and the disciple whom He loved standing nearby, He

said to His mother, "Woman, behold, your son!"
Then He said to the disciple, "Behold, your mother!"
From that hour the disciple took her into his own
household" (John 19:25-27).

There's a power and a majesty about these words which were
spoken as the storm gathered that day, but first we should try to
capture the pathos of the scene. The godly Simeon had foreseen
it by the Spirit of God, when, in taking the infant Jesus from
Mary's arms some 33 years earlier, he had turned to Mary and
said: "Behold, this Child is appointed for the fall and rise of
many in Israel, and for a sign to be opposed - and a sword will
pierce even your own soul - to the end that thoughts from many
hearts may be revealed" (Luke 2:34-35).

It must have seemed a strange thing for Simeon to say. Was
she not the most highly favoured among women? To become
the mother of the long-awaited Messiah - was that not an
indescribable privilege? Of course, it was. But Simeon's words
had sounded ominous. And it had not taken long for Mary's
soul to be pierced with trouble. How hard it must have been for
her to bear the news of Herod's murderous intentions towards
her son, not to mention the trauma of fleeing to Egypt! And
the pain had flared up again when Jesus began to be openly
despised and rejected during his public ministry. But what could
have prepared her for this? To be standing by the cruel tree, the
cross of her son, her mother's heart breaking. Had she not been
the first to plant kisses on that brow - that brow that was now
crowned with thorns? Had she not guided those hands and feet

when as an infant he'd first begun to move around - and now she sees them nailed to the cross? The sword of which Simeon had spoken is now fully plunged into her soul.

As far as the Gospel writers reveal, Mary watched in silence, as the crowds passed by, as the thieves taunted, and the priests jeered and the soldiers paraded their callous indifference. Courageously, Mary stands there, not swooning or wailing, but maintaining her composure. Our Lord had been let down and betrayed in Gethsemane's garden, he'd been denied by Peter, and forsaken by all - but in loving courage Mary stands supportively by his cross. During his mock trial, we read that the high priest had asked Jesus about his disciples (John 18:19). We can't fill in the blanks with any certainty, but we wouldn't have been surprised to hear a sneer: "And where are those followers of yours now?" They were looking for cover from the storm, as far as it affected them. But here was Mary standing by the cross, by this time probably a widow.

I wonder, had this been in the Lord's mind when he'd encountered the widow at Nain - the widow who had been heading out to bury her son? The grief of losing a life-partner had been followed by the loss of a special son. The Lord had been moved with compassion for that dear woman. And now he looks with compassion on his own mother. It seems likely that Joseph had died some time ago - the last record anywhere of him is back at the time when Jesus had been a boy of 12, remaining behind at the Jerusalem temple. Mary, almost certainly a widow, is now losing her special son on whom she'd depended so much. Despite the greatest storm being about to break, bringing with it the most demanding undertaking ever in the history of the world, the Lord's thoughts are still for others. He's already prayed for the soldiers who nailed him there; once again he fulfils not only his own teaching, but the law of Moses - by honoring his mother. Subject to his parents as a youth; he now honors his mother at his death. No doubt - but there's a lesson here. When engaged in the greatest work for God, our Lord himself was considerate of those bound to him by natural family ties. And so we're taught not to fail to provide for our own. Nothing excuses us from that sacred duty - a duty made sacred in no small way by this memorable action of our Lord's, and by these magnificently caring words of his, spoken as the storm closed in upon him.

We've thought of how the disciples had left: him and fled. But at least there was one of them who came back. The disciple John, also known as 'the disciple whom the Lord loved', has made it back to the cross. Perhaps, John, simply because of his frequent description as the disciple whom the Lord loved, would be the very one we'd expect to overcome his fear, to think better of himself, and to return to his Lord at the end. It's one of those quiet consistencies in the Word of God which adds further to our sense of confidence in the total authenticity of the Bible. Of all the disciples, of course, it was John who returned. No rebuke awaits John, only a tremendous honour: to be given responsibility for the care of the Lord's widowed mother. Perhaps, we, too, have known what it is to desert the Lord in some hour of trial which has overtaken us. Here in the case of John, and of how the Lord treated him, we can find real encouragement - encouragement to come back to the Lord, to draw near again to his precious, wounded side.

We can appreciate something of the Lord's wisdom here, for it does seem that John and Mary would be fit companions for each other, having both enjoyed an intimate bond with Christ. From that hour forward, we're told, John took her to his own home. Now, you remember how, on the third day, in the early hours of the resurrection morning, John had outrun Peter to the tomb, where they had found no body. At that moment, in the early dawn, we read about John believing - it became a personal dawning for him of the reality of Jesus' promised resurrection. What does he then do? He went away to his own home, we read (John 20:10). "What's the significance in that?" you may ask. Well, at least in John's case, there's a special significance: for who's in his home – but Mary, the mother of the Lord. At once he would go to share with her the news of what's he's witnessed and come to believe. It's just another of the harmonies of the Bible, giving further credibility to the resurrection event and the reliability of the entire Bible.

CHAPTER FOUR: WHY HAVE YOU FORSAKEN ME?

Seven times we get a mention of the voice of the LORD in the great storm of Psalm 29:

> "The voice of the LORD is upon the waters ...
>
> The voice of the LORD is powerful,
>
> The voice of the LORD is majestic.
>
> The voice of the LORD breaks the cedars...
>
> The voice of the LORD hews out flames of fire.
>
> The voice of the LORD shakes the wilderness...
>
> The voice of the LORD makes the deer to calve
>
> And strips the forests bare ..."
>
> (Psalm 29:39)

That's the dramatic backcloth we're keeping in mind as we gather around the Saviour's cross. While Jesus hung there, the greatest ever storm broke upon him; not a physical storm, but the storm of God's anger against sin. "Deep calls to deep at the roar of your waterfalls; all your breakers and your waves have gone over me ..." (Psalm 42:7). No one ever experienced an application of the psalmist's words like Christ. Overwhelmed with grief, the floodgates of God's wrath against human sin opened against him there, as wave upon wave of sorrow engulfed his soul. He suffered there as no one has ever suffered; and seven times from the cross the Saviour's voice was heard. We now come to the fourth of these sayings, which is recorded in Matthew's Gospel: "Now from the sixth hour there was darkness over all the land until the ninth hour. And about the ninth hour Jesus cried out with a loud voice, saying, "Eli, Eli, lema sabachthani?" that is, "My God, my God, why have you forsaken me?" (Matthew 27:45-46). This is, of course, a quotation from Psalm 22, that great psalm of the cross, which begins:

> "My God, my God, why have you forsaken me? Why are you so far from saving me, from the words of my groaning?" O my God, I cry by day, but you do not answer, and by night, but I find no rest. Yet you are holy, enthroned on the praises of Israel. In you our fathers trusted; they trusted, and you delivered them. To you they cried and were rescued. But I am a worm and not a man, scorned ... and despised by the people. All who see me mock me; they make mouths at me; they wag their heads; "He trusts in the LORD; let him deliver him; let him rescue him, for he delights in him!" (Psalm 22:1-8)

In the great storm which broke upon him at Calvary, our Lord knew what it was to be abandoned by God, for he hung there as the representative of God's rebellious human creation. He was dying the just for the unjust that he might bring us to God (1 Peter 3:18). The Bible could not have made the substitution principle any clearer. It was not for sins which he had done that he groaned upon the tree. Jesus Christ the Righteous, the just, was dying in our place: for us who were unjust in the sight of a holy God, who is our Maker. On the cross, Jesus was forsaken by God, so that all who believe in his sacrifice for them, will never be forsaken by God - and such God forsakenness is the punishment our sins truly deserve. Our rebellious nature makes us want to push God away from us: either in bold defiance or simply by ignoring his claims upon our lives - or even by our patronising self-righteousness. God's sentence for sinners, as revealed in the Bible, is to give us what we ask for: which is separation from himself.

The wages of sin is death, the Bible says, and this spiritual death is the separation of our souls from God. Make no mistake about it: we will exist for ever: but that eternal existence will either be in the presence of God or in separation from God. And since God is the author of life, to be separate from him, is to be separate from all that's good and worthwhile: from all that makes for happiness. God does not want any of us to perish in those terms, so he sent his Son, Jesus, to pay in his death the price we owed as the consequence of our sins. That's what the terrible loneliness of that Godforsaken cross, with its supernatural darkness, was all about.

God had signaled this in advance. The nation of Israel, throughout Old Testament history, had observed a God given ritual. Once a year, when their sins were brought to remembrance, two goats were taken. One was slaughtered at the altar, and the other - after having had all the sins of the people symbolically transferred to it - was led into a desert place and left: behind there. Utterly alone, and forsaken, it was left: to wander and die, bearing the sins of all the people. The New

Testament shows the wonderful grace of God our Judge, when it unmistakably identifies Jesus Christ, God's Son, as the ultimate sin- bearer. He bore none of the moral characteristics of our sins, but he did bear the legal consequences of them, as he hung there, forsaken by God upon the cross, paying in his death the wages of our sin.

This was God's plan of the ages. A plan conceived by him before even the universe had been created. God's Son had been born into humanity with the intention of dying to make our salvation possible. In the first Christian sermon, Peter had said that: "Jesus [was], delivered up according to the definite plan and foreknowledge of God, (but, he went on to address the Jews) you crucified and killed by the hands of lawless men. God raised him up, hosing the pangs of death, because it was not possible for him to be held by it. For David says concerning him,

> "I saw the Lord always before me, for he is at my right hand that I may not be shaken; therefore my heart was glad, and my tongue rejoiced; my flesh also will dwell in hope. For you will not abandon my soul to Hades, or let your Holy One see corruption. You have made known to me the paths of life; you will make me full of gladness with your presence" (Acts 2:23-28).

Peter was quoting from a different psalm which promised that the soul of God's Christ would not be abandoned to Hades, neither would his body see corruption. Jesus' prayer from the cross had, of course, been heard. Here was the answer. Jesus had not been delivered from death, but rather, out of death (Hebrews 5:7 literally). On Friday it looked to all the world like a defeat, but Sunday - resurrection Sunday - was coming, and that would declare Christ's great victory. It reminds me of how the Duke of Wellington's famous victory over Napoleon at Waterloo was announced in England on 18 June, 1815. It was by a system of flag signals from the tower of Winchester Cathedral. The message was spelt: out letter by letter. Onlookers read WELLINGTON DEFEATED ... But then a dense fog rolled in and they lost sight of the flags. The incomplete message spread gloom and despair all the way to London. When the fog finally lifted all the flags were now visible and the full message could be seen to read: WELLINGTON DEFEATED THE ENEMY. The good news spread like wildfire and lifted the people from gloom to gladness.

That story closely parallels the story of the great battle that took place on the cross 2000 years ago when Jesus Christ endured three hours of suffering and then death, while bearing the punishment for our sins. From Friday evening, gloom descended over Jesus followers. As they dealt with his body the message really seemed to them to be reading: JESUS DEFEATED. But come Sunday morning, the gloom had lifted - for there was the empty tomb: and so the full message was JESUS DEFEATED THE ENEMY. Now, God invites us to share the victory of His Son. How? He "commands all ... to repent, because He has appointed a day on which He will judge the world in righteousness by the Man whom He has ordained. He has given assurance of this to all by raising Him from the dead."

Another psalm, Psalm 18, written by king David, after he'd known a time of God's deliverance, contains such dramatic poetry that it seems to point way beyond David and on to

David's greater son, Jesus Christ. I invite you to connect it with the most glorious of all deliverances - when God delivered Jesus out of the death which he suffered for us. The psalm says - and now think of Jesus:

> "I call upon the LORD, who is worthy to be praised, and I am saved from my enemies. The cords of death encompassed me; the torrents of destruction assailed me; the cords of Sheol entangled me; the snares of death confronted me. In my distress I called upon the LORD; To my God I cried for help. From his temple he heard my voice, and my cry to him reached his ears. Then the earth reeled and rocked; the foundations also of the mountains trembled and quaked, because he was angry. Smoke went up from his nostrils, and devouring fire from his mouth; glowing coals flamed forth from him. He bowed the heavens and came down; thick darkness was under his feet. He rode on a cherub and flew; He came swiftly on the wings of the wind.

> He made darkness his covering, his canopy around him, thick clouds dark with water ... He sent from on high, he took me; He drew me out of many waters. He rescued me from my strong enemy and from those who hated me, for they were too mighty for me. They confronted me in the day of my calamity, but the LORD was my support. He brought me out into a broad place; He rescued me, because he delighted in me" (Psalm 18:3-19).

Do you remember the taunt of Jesus' tormentors as they gathered around his cross? Let God rescue him if He delights in him. God did, because he really did delight in him. He delighted in him every day of his earthly life, even as he had delighted in him from all eternity. Well might we say - again with the psalmist – ... exalted be the God of my salvation ... [who] gives great deliverance to ... His anointed" (Psalm 18:46,50).

CHAPTER FIVE: I THIRST

The fifth time the Lord's voice was heard from the cross is recorded for us in John's Gospel where we read in chapter 19: "After this, Jesus, knowing that all things had already been accomplished, to fulfil the Scripture, said, 'I am thirsty.' A jar full of sour wine was standing there; so they put a sponge full of the sour wine upon a branch of hyssop and brought it up to His mouth" (John 19:28-29).

From what immediately follows, we know Jesus said this only a short while before he bowed his head and gave up his spirit. And, if we compare the account in Matthew's Gospel, we can also place it as following on from his previous cry of abandonment: "My God, My God, why have you forsaken Me?" Let's rewind to that point in Matthew's Gospel, chapter 27:

> "From the sixth hour there was darkness over all the land until the ninth hour. And about the ninth hour Jesus cried out with a loud voice, saying, "Eli, Eli, lama sabachthani?" that is, "My God, my God, why have you forsaken me?" And some of the bystanders, hearing it, said, "This man is calling Elijah." And one of them at once ran and took a sponge, filed it with sour wine, and put it on a reed and gave it to him to drink" (Matthew 27:45-48).

We see that it was in response to Jesus' cry expressing his sense of utter desolation that some bystander gave him a drink of sour wine. But John has already told us that this happened after

Jesus said, "I thirst." So, it seems the fourth and fifth utterances were spoken one after the other, and then the wine was given. Which further means, that the cry, "I thirst," was spoken around the time in which the Lord emerged from the strange darkness which had shrouded the scene of the cross from noon until 3 pm. As one preacher (Spurgeon) famously said: "It was midnight at midday." The Lord had been on the cross from 9 am that morning. He had experienced three hours of daylight; and three hours of darkness while hanging there. I was reminded of that fact recently when reading various psalms which talk about 'day and night', often in relation to some deep trial through which the psalmist was passing. One of them is Psalm 42 which reads:

> "As a deer pants for flowing streams, so pants my soul for you, O God. My soul thirsts for God, for the living God. When shall I come and appear before God? My tears have been my food day and night, while they say to me continually, "Where is your God?" Deep calls to deep at the roar of your waterfalls; All your breakers and your waves have gone over me. By day the LORD commands his steadfast love, and at night his song is with me, a prayer to the God of my life." (Psalm 42:1-8).

Those who passed through the experiences behind these words must have endured literal days and nights of weeping and attempts at drawing near to God. At times, God had seemed far away, and their souls thirsted for him, and for a sense of his presence. But, earlier in this booklet, when we recalled the words of verse 7: "Deep calls to deep at the roar of your waterfalls; all your breakers and your waves have gone over me..." We wondered if anyone but the Lord - on the cross - could fully have known this experience of all God's breakers engulfing him? That thought now invites us to apply other parts of this psalm to the greatest of all trials, namely the cross where Jesus died. There was, in effect, day and night there - if we allow for the period of light followed by the period of darkness, the latter of which we might call the 'night season of Calvary'.

What we have seen from the comparison of John's Gospel with Matthew's Gospel - the comparison with which we began this chapter - is that this fifth cry from the cross, when the Saviour said, "I thirst," came as he emerged from the darkness around the ninth hour. We're told it was to fulfil scripture that Jesus cried out, "I thirst." What amazing composure - to think that in all that terrible ordeal, the Lord continued to meditate on the Scriptures, like the blessed man of Psalm 1. You remember how that psalm begins: "Blessed is the man who walks not in the counsel of the wicked, nor stands in the way of sinners, nor sits in the seat of scoffers; but his delight is in the law of the LORD, and on his law he meditates day and night" (Psalm 1:1-2).

In the day and night - in the light and dark periods of the cross - the Lord was meditating on God's Word. Various psalms, it seems, were on his mind, and at this point perhaps, none more so than Psalm 69:

> "Save me, O God! For the waters have come up to my neck. I sink in deep mire, where there is no foothold; I have come into deep waters, and the flood sweeps over me. I am weary with my crying out; my throat

is parched ... More in number than the hairs of my head are those who hate me without cause; mighty are those who would destroy me those who attack me with lies. What I did not steal must I now restore? ... For it is for your sake that I have borne reproach, that dishonor has covered my face. I have become a stranger to my brothers, an alien to my mother's sons.

For zeal for your house has consumed me, and the reproaches of those who reproach you have fallen on me ... I became a byword to them. I am the talk of those who sit in the gate, and the drunkards make songs about me ... Deliver me from sinking in the mire; Let me be delivered from my enemies and from the deep waters. Let not the flood sweep over me, or the deep swallow me up, or the pit dose its mouth over me ... Reproaches have broken my heart, so that I am in despair. I looked for pity, but there was none, and for comforters, but I found none. They gave me poison for food, and for my thirst they gave me sour wine to drink" (Psalm 69:1-21).

In order to get the full force of this fifth saying of the Saviour from the cross, we need to notice its setting: Jesus, knowing that all things had already been accomplished, to fulfil the Scripture, said, "I am thirsty." The reference here is the very point on which we ended our quotation of Psalm 69 a moment ago: for my thirst they gave me sour wine to drink. The predictions of all the previous verses of that particular psalm had already been fulfilled. He'd sunk in the deep mire (v.2); he had been hated without a cause (v.3); he had borne reproach and shame (v.7); he had become a stranger to his brethren (v.8); and a byword, the talk of those in the gate, the song of the drunkards (vv.11,12); and so on ... In his meditation, emerging from Calvary's dark night, he had worked his way down to the twenty-first verse: for my thirst they gave me sour wine to drink.

Only this remained to be fulfilled, and so to bring it about, he cried out, "I thirst!" We say again: what composure! And what an example to us: in enduring this painful trial, the Lord was meditating on God's Word. He had reviewed the entire range of predictions there which had been made concerning the Christ and the death he was to accomplish. Everything that belonged to him in the first 20 verses of Psalm 69 had been fulfilled, it only remained for him to receive the sour wine at this point, and so he cried out, "I thirst."

'The voice of the LORD is majestic'. These words from Psalm 29 seem so appropriate now. The fifth saying is so simple - "I thirst," but in their context they're majestic as we reflect with wonder and with worshipful hearts on our Saviour's composure. Of course, they also emphasize to us the real humanity of the Son of God made flesh so that he might taste death for us on the cross. And they mark the deeper fact that having known God's forsaking for the past three hours of darkness, his deeper thirst now is for the presence of God again, for renewed communion.

What a challenge these words present us with! Christ had fulfilled every scripture in that psalm except one, and now he was anxious to fulfil that as well. Sometimes we're content with partial obedience. If our lives comply with a few scriptures we feel content, but here's the challenge that comes from this fifth saying - a simple cry, but with a profound challenge - is there one scripture, one biblical command which the Holy Spirit is bringing to our attention, one which we've not yet put into effect in our lives? As we consider today the magnificent example of our Saviour, shall we not now resolve together that we simply can't evade that scripture any longer?

There's another time in John's Gospel when it's recorded that, early in his ministry, the Lord sat by a well, thirsty. He asked a woman there to give him a drink, but there's no actual record that he received one. The Lord did go on to say that doing the will of his God and Father was meat and drink to him. What refreshed him that day more than any physical drink, I suggest, was the fact that the sinner woman responded to the will of God in her Iife. In Revelation 3 verse 20, the Lord is pictured as seeking admittance to a place at the table of our heart. If we respond to him, and enjoy the communion he's looking for, then it says not only will we sup with him, but he'll sup with us. By our obedience, and by means of our communion, we can still refresh the Saviour. Shall we enter into his own thirst for communion?

CHAPTER SIX: IT IS FINISHED!

Vance Packard, in his book The Hidden Persuaders, tells of homemakers' problems with cake mixes in the days when they first appeared. The packets of cake-mix contained a warning not to add milk, but to 'just add water'. Some housewives would add milk anyway, as being their own special touch, and would then be disappointed when the cakes or muffins fell. Other cake mixes would also prohibit adding eggs, since eggs and milk had already been added in dry form by the manufacturer. But, women interviewed in the in-depth studies were disturbed: "What sort of cake is it if you just need to add tap water?" they asked incredulously.

It seems we all like to make our own individual contribution to the project in hand. We often don't like it when everything's done for us. It's also true of our salvation. After the preaching of the first Christian sermon, we read in Acts 2:41 concerning the audience reaction that day that: they ... received his word ... And that was it! That was all that was necessary for their salvation: just - if you like - the adding of the water of the Word (Ephesians 5:26), with no contribution of their own. For the Bible plainly teaches salvation is not by our own human works. We're saved by grace through faith (Ephesians 2:8). It is not of works so that none of us may boast. It's not of ourselves. As the hymn says: 'There was no other good enough to pay the price of sin'. And that one was the Lord Jesus Christ. He has done the mighty work. That was what the cross was all about. And so it brings us to the sixth time the Lord's voice was heard from the cross:

"Therefore when Jesus had received the sour wine, He said, "It is finished!" And He bowed His head and gave up His spirit" (John 19:30).

The sixth saying that Jesus spoke from the cross was written down as the single Greek word 'tetelestai', which means, 'It is finished'. It's interesting that ancient receipts for taxes have been recovered which are on papyrus, and have this same Greek word 'tetelestai' written across them. So here's an everyday business use of this word from about the same point in history - and the meaning in that context is very clear: a person's taxes had been 'paid in full.' The tax-collector was satisfied! That helps us to understand that when Jesus spoke the word 'tetelestai' or 'it is finished', it truly means that all the debt owing as a result: of the believer's sins has been paid in full. Jesus paid the price by his death on the cross.

It may be true that many a dying person has said: "I am finished." But Christ said, "It is finished." And there's a world of a difference between the two! Jesus meant all the work of salvation was completed. He had suffered the penalty of God's justice which human sin deserved. I'd like to remind us how closely this sixth saying of the Lord on the cross followed on from the previous utterance. Again, we're reading from John's Gospel: "After this, Jesus, knowing that all things had already been accomplished, to fulfill the Scripture, said, "I am thirsty. "A jar full of sour wine was standing there; so they put a sponge fall of the sour wine upon a branch of hyssop and brought it up to His mouth. Therefore when Jesus had received the sour wine, He said, "It is finished!" And He bowed His head and gave up His spirit" (John 19:28-30).

It's interesting that the word for 'it is finished' is the same one that's used when referring to all things having been accomplished - just a couple of verses earlier. So what was finished? The Law had been fulfilled as never before; and the Messianic prophecies which the Lord had been mentally reviewing were accomplished; but more than that: the work of our salvation was itself completed - with nothing left: for us to do. For "Christ died for our sins, according to the Scriptures", so the apostle Paul told the believers at Corinth (see 1 Corinthians 15:3). "It is finished," was the sixth time our Lord's voice was heard from the cross. It was the sixth out of seven utterances, and we've taken our cue from the Bible in likening the Lord's trial of suffering on the cross to a storm; without doubt the greatest storm ever.

In this book, we've thought about how Psalm 29 is set over against the powerful display of a developing storm. While Jesus hung there, the greatest storm ever broke upon him. He suffered there as no one has ever suffered. The voice of the Lord makes the deer to calve. And in this sixth triumphant cry of the Lord from the storm of Calvary, we too can find our spiritual birth. In his death, can be our birth. The work of salvation is done for us! On our part we must only repent and believe.

In the opening chapter of this book I described a memorable afternoon when a group of us sat together, sharing God's Word. There was a real sense that it was being received as the voice of the living God. Questions came pouring out, and repeatedly we turned to the most relevant Bible verses to provide answers that satisfied hearts which were seriously thirsty. Finally, one lady said, "It's magnificent!" It truly is a magnificent experience whenever we hear God's voice speaking to our heart out of our reading in his Word, the Bible. I pray you'll hear the Lord's voice even now in his word from the cross: "It is finished." Rest by faith in his finished work for your eternal salvation. He wants to be your personal saviour, if only you'll repent and come to him. Perhaps, one of Jesus' own stories will help to emphasise to us again that for salvation, it's not our works, but his alone, that counts:

> "And He also told this parable to some people who trusted in themselves that they were righteous, and viewed others with contempt: "Two men went up into the temple to pray, one a Pharisee and the other a tax collector. "The Pharisee stood and was praying this to himself: 'God, I thank You that I am not like other people: swindlers, unjust, adulterers, or even like this tax collector. 'I fast twice a week; I pay tithes of all that I get.' "But the tax collector, standing some distance away, was even unwilling to lift up his eyes to heaven, but was beating his breast, saying, 'God, be merciful to me, the sinner!' "I tell you, this man went to his house justified rather than the other; for everyone who exalts himself will be humbled, but he who humbles himself will be exalted" (Luke 18:9-14).

This parable was not spoken to play down good works - just to put them in their correct place. We must never trust in our own works and expect God to accept us on the basis of our performance. Suppose a top athlete and an over-weight middle-aged man were about to begin a 100-metre sprint. If the athlete has trained hard and is at the peak of his form, while his opponent has been smoking and drinking, the athlete would be less than honest if he were not confident of his ability to win the contest (although boasting is always inexcusable). When it comes to the work that those who are already Christians are expected to do for God, Paul urges us to adopt the attitude of the athlete in training. There are eternal prizes to be won by careful discipline; whereas, by contrast, carelessness and indulgence may well cause us to be disqualified from service (1 Corinthians 9:24-27). Good works, the Bible says, are to come after, or to accompany, salvation.

But rewards for work well done, important and eternal as they are, are in an altogether different category from salvation and acceptance with God (1 Corinthians 3:10-15). Our acceptance can never depend on our work, nor is salvation a competitive race in which the best performers get the prize. Our very best performance comes far short of God's standards of perfection. But what we can never earn - salvation - God is prepared to give us solely upon the condition of repentance and faith. This is what the story of the tax-collector and the Pharisee shows us. We must all say: "God be merciful to me the sinner!" The comparatively good man (the Pharisee) could not make himself acceptable on any other grounds, and so was, in fact, in no way superior to the most wicked of men.

Whoever we are, or think we are, we need to come 'just as we are', and throw ourselves on the mercy of the Saviour who finished all the work of our salvation for us on the cross. Then, having received God's gift of salvation, we're to do our personal best in service.

"The veil is rent! Lo! Jesus sits

Upon a throne of grace;

The incense which His name emits

Fill all that glorious place.

His precious blood is sprinkled there,

Before and on the throne;

And His own wounds in heav'n declare

His work on earth is done.

'Tis finished!" on the cross He said,

In agonies and blood;

'Tis finished: now He lives to plead

Before the face of God.

'Tis finished!" Here our souls can rest,

His work can never fail;

By Him, our Sacrifice and Priest

We enter through the veil."

CHAPTER SEVEN: I COMMIT MY SPIRIT

For more than twelve hours Christ had been in the hands of sinners just as he had predicted would happen, as early as Matthew chapter 17: "... while they were gathering together in Galilee Jesus said to them, "The Son of Man is going to be delivered into the hands of men; and they will kill Him, and He will be raised on the third day" (Matthew 17:22-23). Then, as the actual time drew near, while in the Garden of Gethsemane, "[Jesus] came to the disciples and said to them, "Are you still sleeping and resting? Behold, the hour is at hand and the Son of Man is being betrayed into the hands of sinners" (Matthew 26:45).

Then, in retrospect, the angels at the empty tomb announced to the women who had come there with their spices: "He is not here, but He has risen. Remember how He spoke to you while He was still in Galilee, saying that the Son of Man must be delivered into the hands of sinful men, and be crucified, and the third day rise again" (Luke 24:6-7). But, now, at the end of the three hours of darkness, Christ spoke his final word from the cross: "... crying out with a loud voice, [He] said, "Father, into Your hands I commit My spirit." Having said this, He breathed His last" (Luke 23:46). He had surrendered himself bodily into the hands of sinners at the time of his arrest in the garden, but now, at the end of his cross ordeal, he committed his spirit into his Father's hands.

Luke, with his focus on Christ the man, records, simply, that he breathed his last. That could be thought of as quite passive. But, Matthew, who presents Christ as King, writes that the Lord literally 'sent forth' or 'dismissed' his spirit, a deliberate action consistent with the authority of a king. It's important for us to notice that, for, earlier in his ministry, the Lord Jesus had said: "For this reason the Father loves Me, because I lay down My life so that I may take it again. No one has taken it away from Me, but I lay it down on My own initiative. I have authority to lay it down, and I have authority to take it up again. This commandment I received from My Father" (John 10:17-18).

Christ's death was absolutely unique. His life was not taken from him. He laid down his life on his own initiative, as an act of his own volition, albeit in obedience to the command he had received from his Father. It's this truth that lies behind the committal of his spirit to his Father. We notice that it's another psalm which this final saying fulfils. It's already clear that the Lord has been meditating on Psalm 22 and Psalm 69 especially, but now it's the turn of Psalm 31:

> "In You, O LORD, I have taken refuge;
>
> Let me never be ashamed;
>
> In Your righteousness deliver me.
>
> Incline Your ear to me, rescue me quickly;
>
> Be to me a rock of strength,
>
> A stronghold to save me.

For You are my rock and my fortress;

For Your name's sake You will lead me and guide me.

You will pull me out of the net which they have secretly laid for me,

For You are my strength.

Into Your hand I commit my spirit."

(Psalm 31:1-5)

This is very precious. For three hours the communion of the Son with the Father had been broken; during those awful three hours he had been forsaken on account of the fact that he was bearing sin for others. But now that storm is over. The bitter cup of suffering has been drained by him. The darkness recedes again. And now the Saviour is once more in communion with his Father - a communion never more to be broken. The first cry from the cross had been, "Father, forgive ..."; the last of the seven sayings is, "Father ... I commit my spirit." Communion restored.

Seven times in relation to the great storm of the cross, the voice of the Lord was heard, reminding us of the seven mentions of 'the voice of the Lord' in Psalm 29. You may remember how we suggested that the marvelous word picture of the development of a great storm there is punctuated seven times by 'the voice of the Lord'.

The voice of the LORD is upon the waters;

The God of glory thunders,

The LORD is over many waters.

The voice of the LORD is powerful,

The voice of the LORD is majestic.

The voice of the LORD breaks the cedars;

Yes, the LORD breaks in pieces the cedars of Lebanon.

He makes Lebanon skip like a calf,

And Sirion like a young wild ox.

The voice of the LORD hews out flames of fire.

The voice of the LORD shakes the wilderness;

The LORD shakes the wilderness of Kadesh.

The voice of the LORD makes the deer to calve

And strips the forests bare;

And in His temple everything says, "Glory!"

(Psalm 29:39)

In this book, we've considered each of the seven sayings of our Saviour, spoken from the cross with its associated terrible storm. We have emphasized the power and the majesty of his voice amid all that storm. Let's conclude our study, then, by referring back to a day in the He of the Lord Jesus when he and his disciples experienced a natural storm on the Sea of Galilee:

"On that day, when evening came, He said to them,
"Let us go over to the other side." Leaving the crowd,
they took Him along with them in the boat, just as He
was; and other boats were with Him. And there arose
a fierce gale of wind, and the waves were breaking over
the boat so much that the boat was already filing up.
Jesus Himself was in the stern, asleep on the cushion;
and they woke Him and said to Him, "Teacher, do
You not care that we are perishing?" And He got up
and rebuked the wind and said to the sea, "Hush,
be still." And the wind died down and it became
perfectly calm. And He said to them, "Why are you
afraid? Do you still have no faith?" They became very
much afraid and said to one another, "Who then is
this, that even the wind and the sea obey Him?"
(Matthew 4:35-41)

Another of the Gospel records has the disciples saying: "What
kind of man is this?" And well they might. And the best answer
to that question was given by the centurion at the foot of Christ's
cross. The Lord's stormy trial of sue ring was over, seven times
his majestic voice had sounded, concluding powerfully with: "...
a loud cry, and [then he] breathed His last. And the veil of
the temple was torn in two from top to bottom. When the
centurion, who was standing right in front of Him, saw the way
He breathed His last, he said, "Truly this man was the Son of
God!" (Matthew 15:37-39).

As we've heard the Lord's voice resound powerfully, majestically, those seven times from the storm of the cross as we've worked our way through this study, I pray that's also been the response of your heart: "Truly this man is the Son of God!" - my magnificent Saviour.

BONUS BOOK - PICTURES OF SALVATION

CHAPTER ONE: THE SLAVE MARKET

Slavery was an accepted way of life in the Roman Empire. So much so that perhaps we could call it an institution in those days. Probably at least a quarter of all people in the empire were slaves. When the apostle Paul was writing his Bible letters, it is estimated that there were something like 20 million slaves just in Italy alone.

Most slaves were domestic helps. The household was made up of husband and wife, their children, and slaves, and was the most important social unit in the Roman Empire. Slaves were involved at every level of life in the household: they took care of finances; prepared the food; dressed the householder and his family; nursed the family when sick; guarded the estate and the family; read poetry; reminded the master of people's names; provided background music at dinner; served as messengers and doorkeepers; and the women were sometimes concubines.

What could be more natural, therefore, than for the apostle Paul to relate the Christian message of salvation to this very common practice and way of life? At that time, people understood the idea of slavery only too well, and a slave would normally dream of obtaining his or her freedom. It's hardly surprising then, that in presenting the Christian message 2,000 years ago, the apostle Paul used the emotive imagery of freedom from slavery. One place where this picture of salvation is clearly used is found in Romans chapter 6, where Paul says: "...thanks be to God that, though you used to be slaves to sin, you wholeheartedly obeyed the form of teaching to which you were entrusted. You have been set free from sin..." (vv.17-18 NIV).

We're all used to the appealing images used by advertisers in selling their product. Rarely, if ever, does the product deliver on the glamorous image that's implied. But with the Christian message it's exactly the opposite! No single human idea or analogy can do it justice! That's why, in this booklet, we'll be looking at the four main pictures Paul used at the Holy Spirit's direction to communicate what it means to experience the spiritual salvation Christianity offers. The picture of human slaves to sin being set free is just one of them - but it's an important one and it's good if we have a bit more background so that we can appreciate it better.

Back in the days of the Roman Empire, people became slaves for a number of reasons. Prisoners of war became slaves. Others were kidnapped and sold into slavery - sometimes as a result of piracy. Another source of slaves was purchase from over the boundaries of the empire. Roman soldiers involved in frontier wars and rebellions had many opportunities to buy prisoners of war as slaves at auctions. But people often became slaves simply because of poverty. Someone who could not pay his debts could be forced into slavery until the debt was paid in service. When a person was no longer able to obtain food and shelter, that person might make a contract to become a slave. Similarly, if a baby wasn't able to be cared for, it could be made the property of a slave owner. Individuals who were part of the slave trade either collected abandoned babies for later sale themselves or bought them from others who found them. The children of slaves also became the possession of the Master. Slavery could also be brought about by conviction in law - as a punishment for a serious crime.

In summary, it's been said that 'slaves were either born or made.' If we pursue the Bible's analogy with slavery as regards our spiritual condition, then we're made to realize that we are 'sinners by nature and by practice'. We inherit a sinful nature from our parents that's traceable all the way back to the disobedience of the first man, Adam. We're all tainted by the original sin (Romans 5:12). This is our in-born tendency to choose to go our own way. As a result we're all sinners by practice, and sin spoils our lives: for all have sinned and fall short of the glory of God, the Bible says (Romans 3:23). And, as Jesus himself said in John 8:34: "everyone who sins is a slave to sin". This is the spiritual slavery that extends to everyone on the planet.

Sin in our lives can show itself to be a harsh master, as when it leads to the destruction of health or the wreck of family life. The life of a Roman slave at times reflected this. While some slaves might have had a better life than that of poor people who were free, others were confined to the private prison attached to most Roman farms. There the slaves were made to work in chains as they cultivated the fields. The prison appears to have been usually underground, lit by narrow windows. The windows were too high from the ground to be touched by the hand. Slaves who had displeased their masters were punished by imprisonment here. It was where all slaves who could not be depended on were housed.

It all reminds me of what Paul had to say in Galatians 3:22 that the Scripture declares that "the whole world is a prisoner of sin, so that what was promised, being given through faith in Jesus Christ, might be given to those who believe" (NIV).

But, in Roman society a slave could buy freedom or someone else could pay a sum of money to obtain a slave's freedom. Freedom was sometimes given as a reward for loyalty. In one case, a woman was set free because she bore four sons who became the master's slaves. Once freedom was attained, the freed person could not be reclaimed as a slave. Sometimes a slave could actually be adopted by the master and inherit equally with the natural sons. This brings us to the good news of Christianity: that all of us who are spiritual slaves to sin can be made free through Jesus Christ. He is the one in whom we have redemption (Ephesians 1:7). The word 'redemption' (Greek: 'apolutrosis') means 'to redeem someone by paying the price for them ... liberation ... by payment of a ransom' (Thayer).

The story of redemption in the New Testament of the Bible can be told in three of its original words. The first ('agorazo': used in 1 Corinthians 6:20; 7:23,30; 2 Peter 2:1; Revelation 5:9) means 'to buy in the slave market'. The way it's applied in the Bible makes the wonderful story of Christianity very clear - that the Lord Jesus came to this earth as man so that he might buy us in the slave market of sin. This slave market represents the degrading situation into which human disobedience had brought us. The second word for redemption (Greek: 'exagorazo'), a word meaning 'to buy out of the slave market', emphasizes that the Christian believer now belongs to the Lord Jesus Christ, since it was he who bought us at a price for himself

(1 Corinthians 6:19-20): Do you not know, Paul asks the Corinthian Christians, "that your body is a temple of the Holy Spirit, who is in you, whom you have received from God? You are not your own; you were bought at a price. Therefore honour God with your body" (NIV).

The redeemed believer on the Lord Jesus is his possession for ever, never again to be put up for sale. The idea of a price having been paid brings us to the third word for redemption (Greek: 'lutroo'), which means 'to liberate by payment of a ransom'. All who repent and believe on Jesus Christ are set free from the guilt and penalty of their sins. This redemption, this forgiveness of sins, is 'through his blood' - for the ransom price paid for sinners was the death of Jesus, the Son of God, when he was crucified outside Jerusalem two thousand years ago in God's plan of salvation: his plan to liberate spiritually all who believe. Let's read more about that tremendous plan from Ephesians 1:5- 7:

> "[God] predestined us to be adopted as his sons through Jesus Christ, in accordance with his pleasure and will - to the praise of his glorious grace, which he has freely given us in the One he loves. In him we have redemption through his blood, the forgiveness of sins, in accordance with the riches of God's grace" (NIV).

Our concluding thought concerns the fact that believers on the Lord Jesus now have an obligation to live for him. He is the one who has bought them out of the slave market of sin. This is how Paul puts it in writing to his Christian friends in Rome: "You have been set free from sin and have become slaves to righteousness ... But now that you have been set free from sin and have become slaves to God, the benefit you reap leads to holiness, and the result is eternal life. For the wages of sin is death, but the gift of God is eternal life in Christ Jesus our Lord" (Romans 6:18-23 NIV).

CHAPTER TWO: THE LAW COURTS

In the previous chapter we were thinking about how slavery was an everyday fact of life, and how the apostle Paul, directed by the Holy Spirit, drew upon this background in one of the main pictures of salvation he used: that of being set free from sin's spiritual slavery. It's a different kind of freedom we want to explore now. Not so much ethical, but legal.

We now turn our searchlight on another favourite source of illustration for Paul. In doing so, we make our way from the slave-market to the law courts. Paul was certainly aware of his legal rights as a Roman citizen. Once, he escaped a flogging because he asserted those rights. Paul had an incisive mind, and in his own defence at times he went head-to-head with the best advocates of the day (for example in Acts 24)!

Perhaps after its armies, the Roman legal system was the greatest strength of the Roman Empire. The rights of citizens were firmly upheld in the courts. Then, as today, cases in court were decided by argument between lawyers, and judgements by elected magistrates were based on earlier decisions. Roman law has had a significant influence on legal systems down to the present day - certainly in Europe. Sometimes when sharing the Christian message, Paul seems to use legal language and forensic terms, his reasoning no doubt reflecting the legal processes of the time. It's worth looking at this, because we believe the Holy Spirit was directing Paul in his choice of the language and terms we find in the Bible.

When writing to his Christian friends at the very heart of the empire in Rome, Paul argues that all - both Gentile (non-Jew) and Jew - have sinned. As we read through to the end of the third chapter of his letter to the Romans, it's as if the death sentence has already been passed (for such are the wages of sin) and we, the prisoners, are helplessly awaiting the inevitable on death row. There's a mounting sense of dread suspense as if the footsteps of the executioner are getting nearer and nearer to the cell on death row where the prisoner is housed. As we read verses from these chapters, one after another, think of them as footsteps drawing nearer to a convicted prisoner: "For the wrath of God is revealed from heaven against all ungodliness" (Romans 1:18), "God gave them over to a depraved mind, to do those things which are not proper" (Romans 1:28), "Therefore you have no excuse" (Romans 2:1), "The judgment of God rightly falls upon those who practice such things" (Romans 2:2), "But because of your stubbornness and unrepentant heart you are storing up wrath for yourself in the day of wrath and revelation of the righteous judgment of God, who will render to each person according to his deeds" (Romans 2:5-6).

All these verses fall like heavy footsteps, sounding louder and louder...as it is written, "There is none righteous, not even one" (Romans 3:10), "All have turned aside...there is none who does good (Romans 3:12), "... because by the works of the Law no flesh will be justified in His sight; for through the Law comes the knowledge of sin" (Romans 3:20), "For all have sinned and fall short of the glory of God ..." (Romans 3:23).

These verses fall upon our ears like the unrelenting footsteps of the executioner as he draws ever nearer to our condemned cell. Condemned, convicted, and broken by the realization that all this is true, we sit and await the inevitable. It's as if we hear the hand of the executioner begin to turn the door handle...

Then suddenly at verse 24 of the third chapter, it's as if the cell door is suddenly flung open and we read: being justified as a gift by His grace through the redemption which is in Christ Jesus. Try to visualize it with me. It's as though light suddenly and unexpectedly pours into our cell. In a dramatic pronouncement we're declared free to go. Free! Made free, and not simply forgiven, but reckoned 'Not guilty'! Who could blame us for standing there blinking with surprise? This is no jail-break. There's no miscarriage of justice involved. Justice has been satisfied because of the work of Christ! Paul continues by explaining that Jesus Christ, the Son of God, hung and died on the cross two thousand years ago for "the demonstration ... of [God's] righteousness ... so that [God] would be just and the justifier of the one who has faith in Jesus" (Romans 3:26).

It's precisely this language of justification that's taken from the legal system. It's the declaring of someone as righteous (or just). The word is a forensic one, and one that's not used in Greek literature for making righteous. Instead, it is used for the reckoning of righteousness. It consists of the non-reckoning of sins. Romans chapter 4 is a good place to see that. In the language of one Bible version we read there:

"Abraham believed God, and it was credited to him as righteousness." Now to the one who works, his wage is not credited as a favor, but as what is due. But to the one who does not work, but believes in Him who justifies the ungodly, his faith is credited as righteousness, just as David also speaks of the blessing on the man to whom God credits righteousness apart from works: "... Blessed is the man whose sin the Lord will not take into account." (Romans 4:3-8)

We know what it means to receive a credit (payment) on some statement of account. In a different context we may even have experienced getting credit for something we haven't done, perhaps credit we don't deserve. But isn't it amazing to think that, knowingly, God is prepared to credit us with something we don't deserve - to credit that we haven't earned! On the evidence of our faith alone (just as it was with Abraham) God will credit us with righteousness, meaning our sins will not be reckoned against us. Suddenly our guilt, our debt, the debit balance of our account with God, is transformed into credit. It is pure grace, activated on our part by personal faith, as verse 16 of Romans 4 says: "For this reason it is by faith, in order that it may be in accordance with grace."

Returning to the story of Abraham, Paul adds: "Therefore it was also credited to him as righteousness. Now not for his sake only was it written that it was credited to him, but for our sake also, to whom it will be credited, as those who believe in Him who raised Jesus our Lord from the dead, He who was delivered over because of our transgressions, and was raised because of our justification" (Romans 4:22-25 NASB).

So this is another important picture of salvation, drawn up for us by the Spirit of God, against the background of the Roman - and subsequent - legal systems. In this picture we have seen that the Bible word 'justification' is the legal and formal acquittal from guilt by God as Judge; it's the declaring of a verdict of 'not guilty'. How good it is to know that we are no longer guilty before a holy God as a result of having put our faith in Jesus Christ, his son! And what a wonderful pronouncement by God the Judge - the pronouncement of the sinner as righteous, whenever he or she believes on the Lord Jesus Christ! As someone has pointed out, there's an easy way to think of the word 'justified': simply sound it out as "just-as-if-I'd never sinned"!

CHAPTER THREE: THE TEMPLE SHRINE

At the start of this new chapter let's look again at Paul's New Testament letter which he wrote to his friends in Rome. For the four pictures of salvation which are the theme of this booklet can all be found well documented in the apostle Paul's letter. In Romans chapter 3 verses 24 and 25, after telling us that we have all sinned, the Holy Spirit of God through Paul continues with the good news of salvation:

> "being justified as a gift by His grace through the redemption which is in Christ Jesus; whom God displayed publicly as a propitiation in His blood through faith. This was to demonstrate His righteousness, because in the forbearance of God He passed over the sins previously committed." (Romans 3:24-25)

There are three descriptions there of the work Jesus Christ, the Son of God, performed when he died on a Roman cross just outside the city of Jerusalem some two thousand years ago. What took place there is first of all viewed as 'redemption'. That was the subject of the first chapter in the booklet. It's a commercial term drawn from the marketplace where in the society of those days humans as well as other goods were bought and sold. We understood redemption as the idea of someone being bought out of the slave market and being given their freedom - one picture of our salvation as being from the slavery of sin.

Another way in which the cross of Christ was viewed in the two verses we read was as a 'demonstration' - of God's justice. Previously, Paul explains, God had in his forbearance passed over sins. But the cross stands for all time to make it absolutely clear that God never at any time had the intention of ignoring them, far less condoning them. The cross was planned in advance as the demonstration of his justice. The language at this point is legal language, of course, borrowed from the law court, and we spent time on that picture of salvation in our previous study. Now, we're going to be occupied with the third view of the cross that's found within the span of verses 24 and 25 of Romans chapter 3. The third view of the cross is contained in the description of what happened there as being a 'propitiation'. This is an important Bible word, but one that perhaps needs even more by way of explanation than the others.

If the word 'redemption' was one which was then in use in the marketplaces; and if the word 'justification' would have been encountered in the law courts; then the word 'propitiation' would have been commonly used in the pagan temples of the time. In that setting it meant to placate or to appease the angry gods which the pagans acknowledged.

At first we might think there can be no connection between this idea of turning away anger and the biblical teaching of Christianity. After all, the living and true God who is our creator is presented to us in the pages of the Bible as being an unchanging God, certainly not fickle and petty-minded, which was how the pagans viewed their gods. Their gods were always needing to be placated - but let's take a closer look...

In these verses in Romans chapters 1, 2 and 3, Paul's describing God's solution for the human predicament, which is not only sin, but also God's wrath upon sin. Perhaps today the idea of an angry God is considered less than a Christian point of view. But if our property is defaced or our loved ones come under an unprovoked attack, we would expect to feel righteous indignation against the wrong done to us. It's what we then do with that anger that can involve sinful behaviour. God's righteous anger is never uncontrolled.

So we're going to have to identify exactly how this term 'propitiation' is different within a Christian understanding. The reason why it's necessary, and the one who initiates it, and even the means by which it's performed are all radically different within Christianity compared with the way in which propitiation was understood in pagan temples and the background customs of New Testament times. Remember by propitiation we mean the turning away of God's anger.

Among the pagans the need for propitiation arose because they understood the gods to be angry simply because they were a bad-tempered bunch, always subject to mood swings. The Christian explanation of the need for turning away God's anger could not be more different. God's anger, or wrath, is his consistent antagonism against sin, his hatred of anything that's morally evil. God's holy nature cannot accommodate any wrongdoing. It remains hostile to anything which misses the mark of his glorious perfection.

Next we think of how the pagans assumed that only they could appease their gods, after all it was they who had somehow offended them. In the Christian setting, however, the Bible plainly teaches us that we cannot appease God's righteous anger; nothing we can do can make ourselves acceptable to God. But it goes on to tell us that God has done what we could not do. This is how the apostle John puts it: "In this the love of God was made manifest among us, that God sent his only Son into the world, so that we might live through him. In this is love, not that we have loved God but that he loved us and sent his Son to be the propitiation for our sins." (1 John 4:9-10)

What we couldn't do, God has done. At the cross God's anger was turned away from us and directed at himself in the person of his son, Jesus Christ. We need to be very clear about the fact that both the initiative and the action of this propitiation lay with God. Then there's the means by which propitiation was made. The pagans bribed their gods with various sweetmeats. This was very different from the sacrificial system we read about in the Old Testament, because even in it the people were made to understand they were giving back to God from what he had given them in the first place. A verse in Leviticus made that clear: "For the life of the flesh is in the blood, and I have given it for you on the altar to make atonement for your souls, for it is the blood that makes atonement by the life" (Leviticus 17:11).

In the New Testament it's even clearer that the work of salvation and the means by which God's wrath is turned away from us is not our own doing, but is all of God's grace. We return to our opening text from Romans chapter 3: "being justified as a gift by His grace through the redemption which is in Christ

Jesus; whom God displayed publicly as a propitiation in His blood through faith. This was to demonstrate His righteousness, because in the forbearance of God He passed over the sins previously committed." (Romans 3:24-25)

So there we have it: a third biblical picture of salvation. In contrast with the previous two we've looked at where the word concerned, be it redemption or justification, had an agreed meaning which could simply be applied to Christian teaching œ we've seen that the language of the temple shrines (in particular, this word propitiation) had to be redefined.

Finally, it's worth noting that Paul addressed this letter to Christian believers, calling them 'saints' (Romans 1:7); in other words, those who had been sanctified. This terminology was also one that had a background in the pagan Greek religions. There it meant 'devoted to the gods' (according to Liddell and Scott). For example, if a Greek worshipper brought a gift to his god, he devoted it to that god. The gift became holy in that sense. There's no thought of purity in the word, but only the idea of being set apart from common use so as to be devoted to the gods. Paul can biblically describe every Christian believer as a saint in the sense that the Holy Spirit has taken each believing sinner and set him or her apart for God by placing them 'in Christ'.

What's more, corresponding to that, there's to be a practical holiness - or sanctification - increasingly seen in the purity of the believer's life for the Lord Jesus. There again we have to part company with the pagan background of the word, for in the

Greek thought of holiness there was no sense of morality, for the pagan religions of that time were in fact rather immoral. God's thoughts are indeed much higher than our own!

CHAPTER FOUR: THE FAMILY CIRCLE

To introduce our fourth and final picture of salvation, we now need to introduce ourselves to what would have been in many respects a fairly typical family. So far we've seen how Paul's pictures of salvation were drawn from the marketplace, the law courts and the pagan temple shrines. For this last picture we come much closer to home - into the circle of family life. So let's meet the family. Dad and Mum appear to be comfortably well off; well-liked and, what's more, they're committed Christians. They host the gatherings of the local church in their own home, and they've a son who's active in serving the Lord.

Sometime back there was real drama in the household when a domestic help ran off - with how much of the 'silverware' we're not entirely sure. The fuss soon died down, until one Sunday in church there was a dramatic announcement which contained some startling news ... Perhaps, by this stage, you may have a feeling that you already know this family from somewhere. Perhaps you do - from the pages of the New Testament! Dad is Philemon and Apphia is his wife. The Church of God at Colossae (in first century Turkey) meets in their home. Their son, we believe, is Archippus whom no less that the apostle Paul respects as a 'fellow soldier'. It was from this household that Onesimus ran off - and didn't stop running for a 1,000 miles until he reached Rome! That was quite a marathon, but it was necessary because his crime was punishable by death under Roman law.

Actually, it seems there might have been two letters to be read to the church that Sunday morning we referred to. They are the Bible letters we now know as Colossians and Philemon. Have you ever wondered why the letter to Philemon is included in the Bible? It's only 25 verses long, with no deep meaning or direct teaching; and it's generally ignored even by the Christian public. One good reason it's there is to illustrate how we can mend broken relationships. It's also a prime example of how we should put Bible teaching into immediate daily practice.

We don't fully know why Onesimus ran away. In part, it could have been to escape the gospel at home. Perhaps there's a clue (v.18) that he had stolen 'something for his journey'. Facing a death sentence, he just kept on running. A big city like Rome was just the place to 'lose himself'. In fact, it was there that he 'found himself' - through meeting Paul and through becoming a born-again Christian. Perhaps Onesimus either fell into trouble in Rome or found employment in the prison service. Whatever the case, it was in prison he met the apostle Paul - and Epaphras. He could hardly have expected to meet Epaphras who was from his hometown of Colossae 1,000 miles away, but God's providence is a wonderful thing! It's even possible that Epaphras was acquainted with some of the facts concerning Philemon and his runaway slave who was now standing before them.

We can be sure that Paul, in conversation with Onesimus, lost no time in telling him about his need to know Jesus Christ as Saviour. Onesimus listened and by God's grace, responded. So, like Abraham, Paul had the joy of having a son in his old age - a spiritual one! And like Joseph, he had been made fruitful in trying conditions! It was all going to work together for good:

not only with Onesimus' saving faith in Christ, but with his return and reconciliation to his master! For Paul was sending him back to Colossae to be reconciled with Philemon. But he wasn't sending him back empty-handed: he and Tychicus would be carrying two letters that are now found in our Bibles.

The two letters - to the Colossians and to Philemon - were written and delivered at the same time (Colossians 4:7-9). The letter to the Colossians has the direct teaching about Christ and Christian relationships; while the letter to Philemon (which I imagine the whole church heard too) simply contained a strikingly-timed appeal to put it into immediate practice in the case of Onesimus who came with them! Very relevant teaching for exactly that kind of real life situation is found in the letter to the Colossians: "there is no distinction between ... slave and freeman ... as those who have been chosen of God ... put on a heart of compassion, ... forgiving each other, whoever has a complaint against anyone; just as the Lord forgave you, so also should you" (Colossians 3:11-13 NASB).

And if that seemed to have a message applicable to Philemon, a little later on there was a message that was just as applicable to Onesimus, the runaway slave: "Slaves, in all things obey those who are your masters on earth, not with external service, as those who merely please men, but with sincerity of heart, fearing the Lord" (Colossians 3:22 NASB).

How often have we heard Bible teaching and been slow to put it into practice? They had an immediate opportunity brought before them in the second letter! In the more personal letter to Philemon, Paul urged Philemon to apply the teaching on reconciliation and forgiveness. What this demonstrates - quite dramatically - is the fact that reconciliation is readily associated with, and frequently needed, in family life (or life within a household) which in those days included domestic slaves. Reconciliation with one another is one thing (albeit an important matter) but Paul spoke of our need of salvation in terms of our need to be reconciled with God. In his second letter to Corinth he put it like this:

> "If anyone is in Christ, he is a new creature; the old things passed away; behold, new things have come. Now all these things are from God, who reconciled us to Himself through Christ and gave us the ministry of reconciliation, namely, that God was in Christ reconciling the world to Himself, not counting their trespasses against them, and He has committed to us the word of reconciliation. Therefore, we are ambassadors for Christ, as though God were making an appeal through us; we beg you on behalf of Christ, be reconciled to God." (2 Corinthians 5:17-20)

So reconciliation is another of the major words that explain and illustrate the Christian message of salvation. Perhaps we're reminded of another story told by Jesus, not of the runaway slave, but of the runaway son. In Luke chapter 15 we read how this young man demanded his share of his father's inheritance and then left home and spent it wastefully. Soon he was deserted by the friends he had while his money lasted, and being in debt, he was reduced to feeding pigs. It was there he came to his senses and decided to return to his father and throw himself on his mercy. If only he might hope that his father would allow him to live in the lean-to behind the cowshed, he would be prepared to earn his passage among the hired hands on his father's farm. But when he turns around and goes to meet his father and blurts out his confession, "I have sinned", he discovers that his father has been waiting for him and he is welcomed back as a son with great rejoicing.

Sin (our natural tendency to go our own way) is the thing that spoils our lives. It separates us from God. We are estranged from him and our debt against him accumulates. When God's Spirit works in our hearts we, too, come to our senses, and whenever we throw ourselves upon God's mercy, asking for the forgiveness that's found in Jesus Christ, his son, we discover something more than we could ever have expected: God as a Father who welcomes us into his own family.

When we turn from our sins and turn to God, when we receive Jesus Christ by faith, we find ourselves reconciled to God - and born again as a child of God (John 1:12), and adopted as a legal heir of a glorious heavenly inheritance (Ephesians 1:5; 1 Peter 1:3-4). Isn't that wonderful? In the Roman world a child was formally adopted at maturity, in an act that officially declared him as legal heir to his father. It also wasn't unheard of in the Roman world for a household slave to be adopted. Paul's language in Galatians chapter 4 captures something of this when he says:

> "... as long as the heir is a child, he does not differ at all from a slave although he is owner of everything, but he is under guardians and managers until the date

set by the father. So also we, while we were children, were held in bondage under the elemental things of the world. But when the fullness of the time came, God sent forth His Son, born of a woman, born under the Law, so that He might redeem those who were under the Law, that we might receive the adoption as sons." (Galatians 4:1-5)

Reconciliation and adoption: two great Bible words explaining the Christian message of salvation as the mending of our broken relationship with God. And with them we conclude this booklet on pictures of salvation - one which has seen us visit the marketplace, the law courts and the temple shrines, as well as the more homely family setting.

Did you love *Stronger Than the Storm - The Last Words of Jesus*? Then you should read *Deepening Our Relationship With Christ* by Brian Johnston!

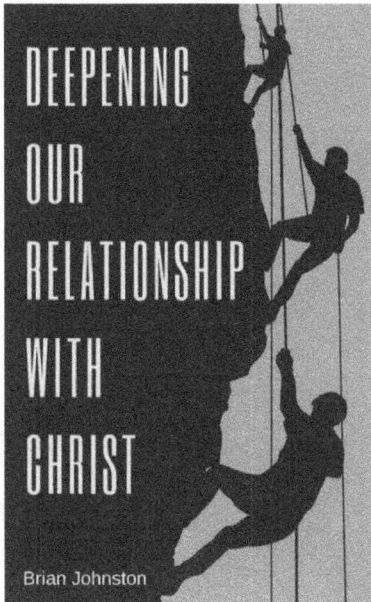

The first step in our relationship with Jesus is accepting Him as our Saviour - but that's just the beginning! In this short book, Brian Johnston expounds 8 important ways that every Christian should deepen their personal relationship with Christ.

1. In being in union with Him
2. In being built on Him
3. In being United by and with Him
4. In following Him
5. In owning Him as Head of the Body
6. In being added alongside Him

7. In being subject to Him as Son over God's House
8. In remembering Him

Also by Brian Johnston

Healthy Churches - God's Bible Blueprint For Growth
Hope for Humanity: God's Fix for a Broken World
First Corinthians: Nothing But Christ Crucified
Bible Answers to Listeners' Questions
Living in God's House: His Design in Action
Christianity 101: Seven Bible Basics
Nights of Old: Bible Stories of God at Work
Daniel Decoded: Deciphering Bible Prophecy
A Test of Commitment: 15 Challenges to Stimulate Your
Devotion to Christ
John's Epistles - Certainty in the Face of Change
If Atheism Is True...
8 Amazing Privileges of God's People: A Bible Study of Romans
9:4-5
Learning from Bible Grandparents
Increasing Your Christian Footprint
Christ-centred Faith
Mindfulness That Jesus Endorses
Amazing Grace! Paul's Gospel Message to the Galatians
Abraham: Friend of God
The Future in Bible Prophecy
Unlocking Hebrews
Learning How To Pray - From the Lord's Prayer

About the Bush: The Five Excuses of Moses
The Five Loves of God
Deepening Our Relationship With Christ
Really Good News For Today!
A Legacy of Kings - Israel's Chequered History
Minor Prophets: Major Issues!
The Tabernacle - God's House of Shadows
Tribes and Tribulations - Israel's Predicted Personalities
Once Saved, Always Saved - The Reality of Eternal Security
After God's Own Heart : The Life of David
Jesus: What Does the Bible Really Say?
God: His Glory, His Building, His Son
The Feasts of Jehovah in One Hour
Knowing God - Reflections on Psalm 23
Praying with Paul
Get Real ... Living Every Day as an Authentic Follower of Christ
A Crisis of Identity
Double Vision: Hidden Meanings in the Prophecy of Isaiah
Samson: A Type of Christ
Great Spiritual Movements
Take Your Mark's Gospel
Total Conviction - 4 Things God Wants You To Be Fully Convinced About
Esther: A Date With Destiny
Experiencing God in Ephesians
James - Epistle of Straw?
The Supremacy of Christ
The Visions of Zechariah
Encounters at the Cross
Five Sacred Solos - The Truths That the Reformation Recovered

Kingdom of God: Past, Present or Future?
Overcoming Objections to Christian Faith
Stronger Than the Storm - The Last Words of Jesus
Fencepost Turtles - People Placed by God
Five Woman and a Baby - The Genealogy of Jesus
Pure Milk - Nurturing New Life in Jesus
Jesus: Son Over God's House
Salt and the Sacrifice of Christ
The Glory of God
The Way: Being a New Testament Disciple
Power Outage - Christianity Unplugged
Windows to Faith: Insights for the Inquisitive
Home Truths
60 Minutes to Raise the Dead

About the Author

Born and educated in Scotland, Brian worked as a government scientist until God called him into full-time Christian ministry on behalf of the Churches of God (www.churchesofgod.info). His voice has been heard on Search For Truth radio broadcasts for over 30 years (visit www.searchfortruth.podbean.com) during which time he has been an itinerant Bible teacher throughout the UK and Canada. His evangelical and missionary work outside the UK is primarily in Belgium and The Philippines. He is married to Rosemary, with a son and daughter.

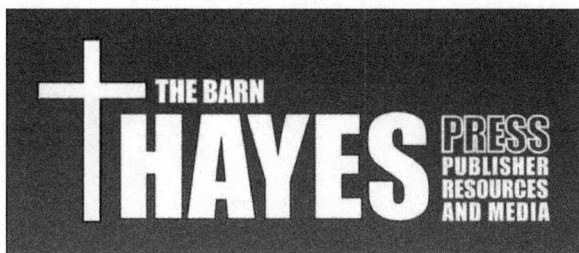

About the Publisher

Hayes Press (www.hayespress.org) is a registered charity in the United Kingdom, whose primary mission is to disseminate the Word of God, mainly through literature. It is one of the largest distributors of gospel tracts and leaflets in the United Kingdom, with over 100 titles and hundreds of thousands despatched annually. In addition to paperbacks and eBooks, Hayes Press also publishes Plus Eagles Wings, a fun and educational Bible magazine for children, and Golden Bells, a popular daily Bible reading calendar in wall or desk formats. Also available are over 100 Bibles in many different versions, shapes and sizes, Bible text posters and much more!

www.ingramcontent.com/pod-product-compliance
Lightning Source LLC
Chambersburg PA
CBHW020518030426
42337CB00011B/441